Sewing by Hand

By Christine Hoffman

Pictures by Harriett Barton

HarperCollinsPublishers

For my mother

Susan Whitman Oates

—C.H.

For my aunt

Doris Wyatt Sutton

—H.B.

Contents

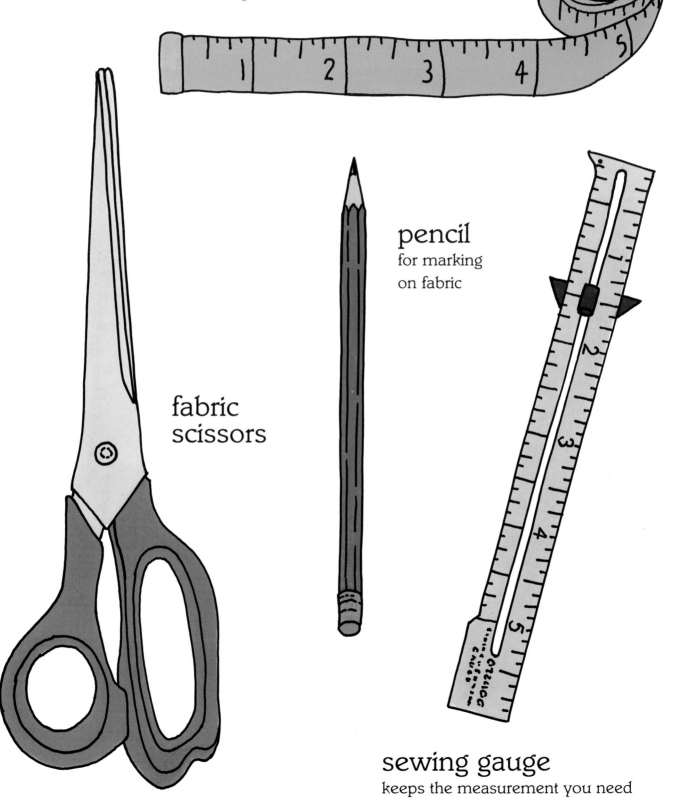

tape measure

used for measuring fabric.
A standard tape measure
is 60 inches long.

1 2 3 4 5

fabric
scissors

pencil

for marking
on fabric

sewing gauge

keeps the measurement you need

4

Tools

pins
used for holding fabric
in place while sewing

pincushion
a safe place to keep pins

needles
There are many different
sizes and shapes of needles.
"Sharps" are best
for hand sewing.

**embroidery
scissors**
nice to have
for snipping thread,
but not necessary

thimble
fits on middle finger
of sewing hand and
helps push needles
through fabric without
pricking fingers

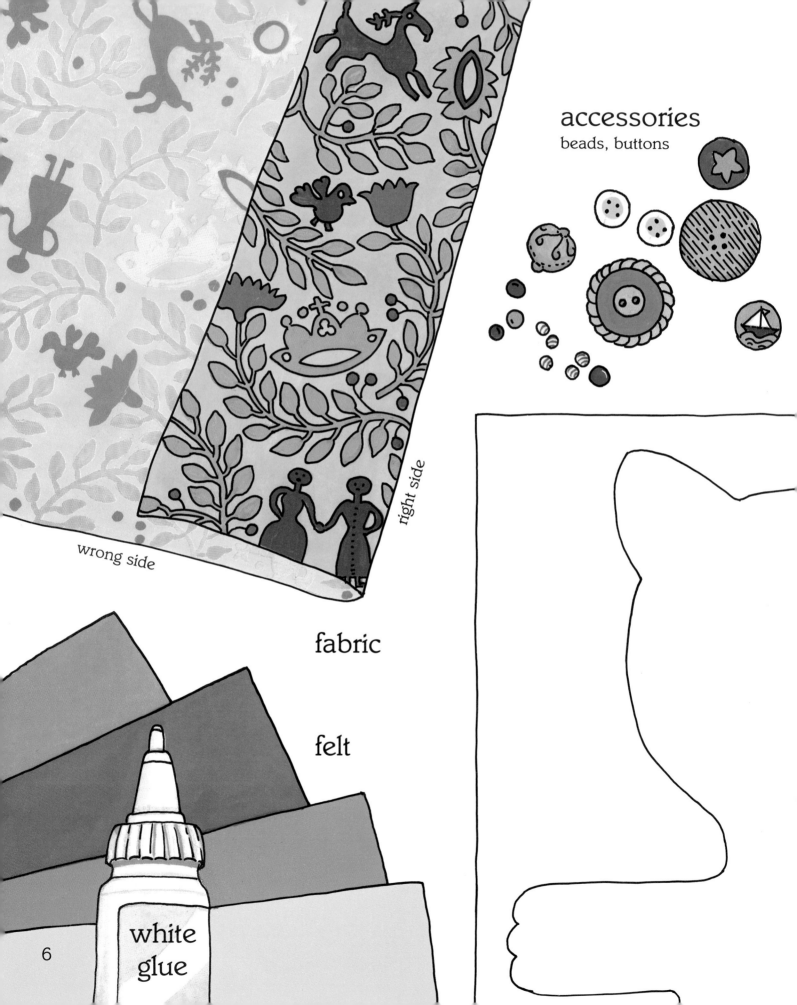

right side

wrong side

accessories
beads, buttons

fabric

felt

white
glue

6

Materials

stuffing
polyester fiberfill,
sold in fabric and
craft stores

dressmaking
thread
cotton or
polyester

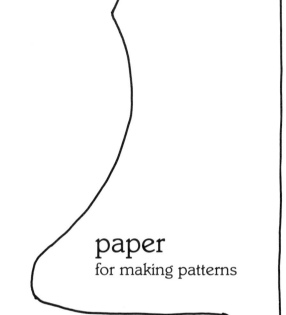

paper
for making patterns

lentil beans

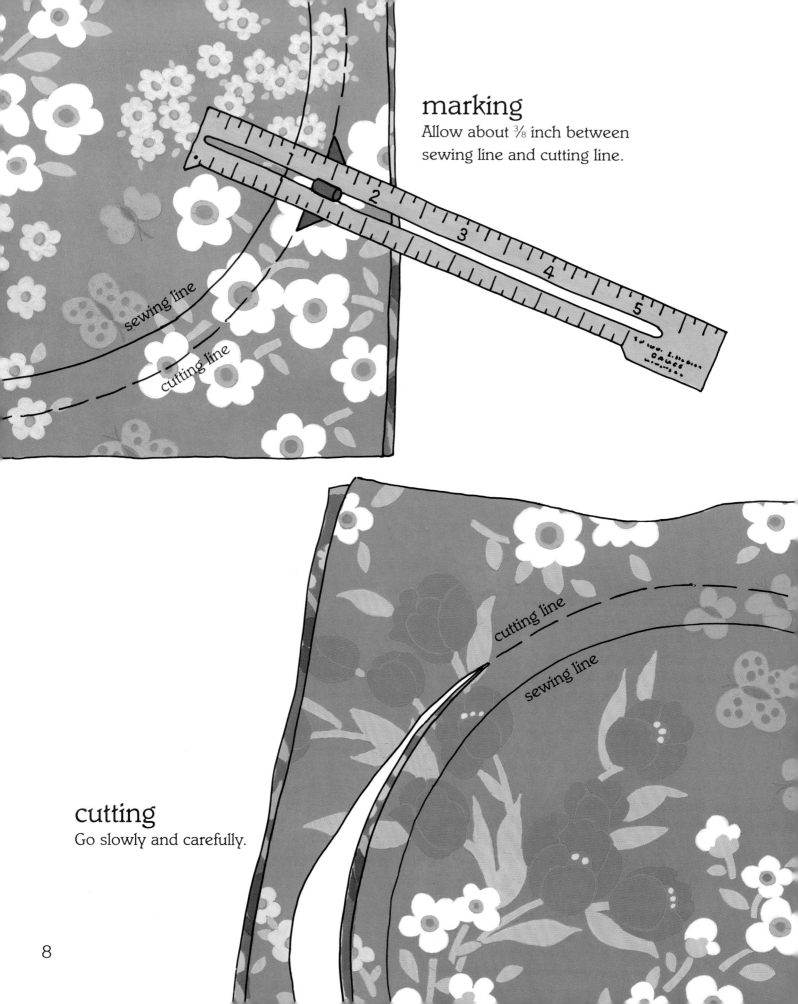

marking
Allow about ⅜ inch between sewing line and cutting line.

sewing line

cutting line

cutting line

sewing line

cutting
Go slowly and carefully.

Sewing Skills

marking • For each project, you will be marking your fabric by drawing a sewing line and a cutting line to use as guides.

cutting • Cut fabric on a large table or on the bare floor. Follow the cutting line and keep the fabric flat.

threading a needle • Cut a piece of thread about the length of your arm. Hold your hands steady by leaning one hand against the other and push the end of the thread through the eye of the needle. If the end of the thread starts to fray, you need to recut or lick it, and then try again.

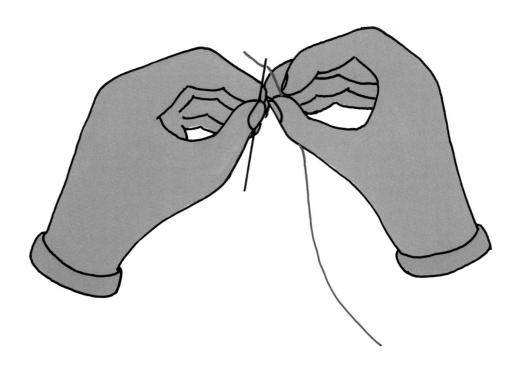

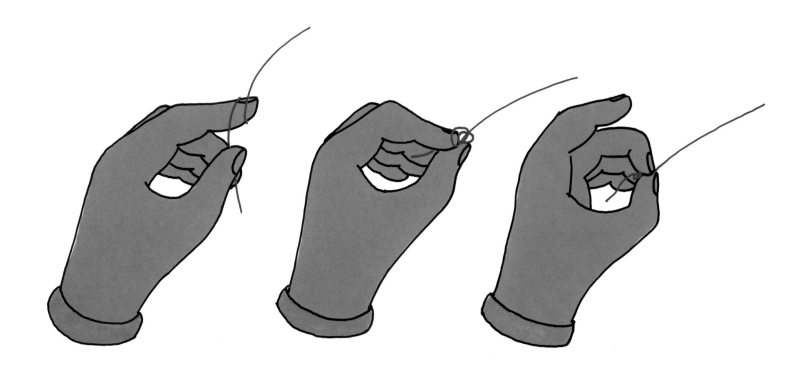

beginning knot • Start by threading a needle. Wind one end of the thread around the tip of your forefinger a few times. Push your thumb forward, twirling the thread. Slip your forefinger out of the loop. Push down on the loop with your middle finger and pull tight. Snip off the end of the thread with your scissors.

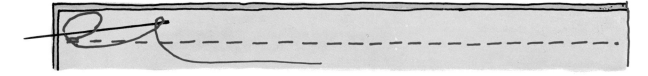

ending knot • Sew two small stitches, one on top of the other. Run the needle and thread all the way under these stitches. Let the thread form a loose loop. Put the needle and thread through this loop. Pull tight. Run the thread under the stitches again, catch the new loop, and pull tight again. Cut off the extra thread.

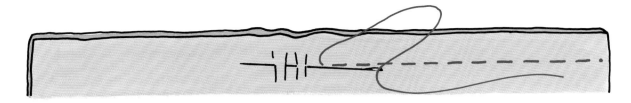

running stitch

running stitch • Thread a needle and make a beginning knot. Push the needle in and out of the fabric twice. Each stitch should be about ⅛ inch long. Pull your thread all the way through so that the beginning knot catches on the fabric. Pull the thread firmly, but not so tight that your fabric puckers. Secure with an ending knot.

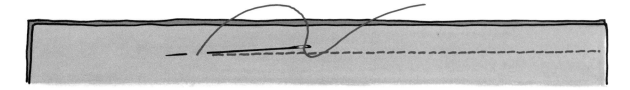

backstitch

backstitch • Thread a needle and make a beginning knot. From the back side of the cloth, push the needle into the fabric and pull through so that the knot catches on the fabric. Insert the needle about ⅛ inch behind where the needle first came through. Bring the needle back through the fabric about ⅛ inch in front of where your thread first came through. Continue making a line of stitches, starting each stitch by inserting the needle ⅛ inch behind its last exit point and then bringing it through ⅛ inch in front. Secure with an ending knot.

overhand stitch

overhand stitch • Hide the knot by inserting a threaded needle between two pieces of fabric and pull it all the way through one layer of the fabric so the knot is pulled tight. Take a stitch through both pieces close to the knot, and pull firmly. Continue making small, even stitches through both layers of fabric along the gap. Always insert the needle on the same side and pull it out on the other side. When you come to the end of the gap, make a secure ending knot. Snip off any extra thread.

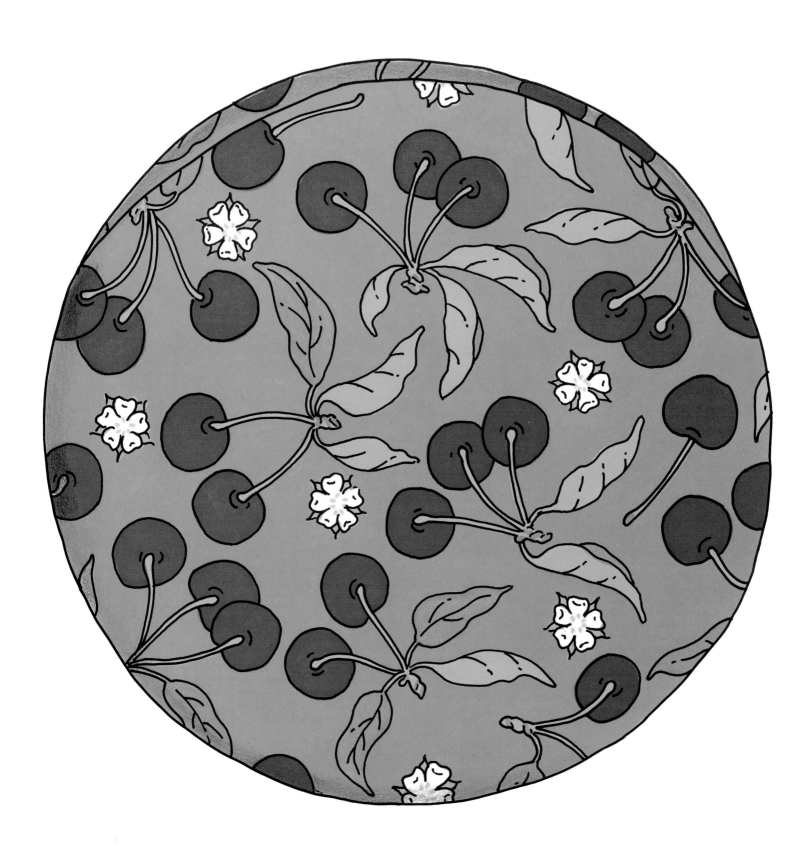

Circle Pillow

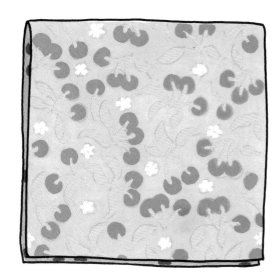

You will need: • ½ yard of fabric • needle • thread • scissors • pins • fiberfill stuffing • pencil • tape measure • large bowl (about 15 inches wide)

1 Lay your fabric out flat on a smooth surface. Fold it into a double layer with right sides facing each other. Smooth out any buckles or folds.

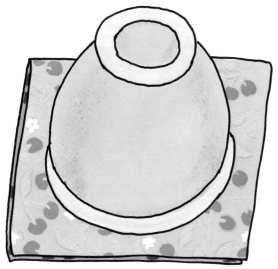

2 Place the bowl upside down on the fabric and carefully trace around the rim with a pencil. This will be the sewing line.

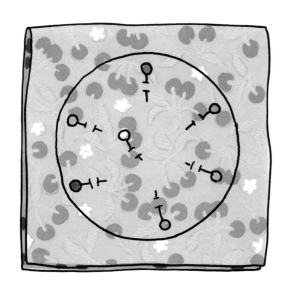

3 Put the bowl aside, and pin the fabric together inside the circle.

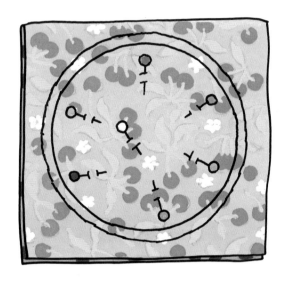

4   Make a small mark ⅜ inch out from the sewing line. Repeat, making a mark about every inch all the way around the circle. Then draw a line connecting all the marks. This new outer circle is the cutting line.

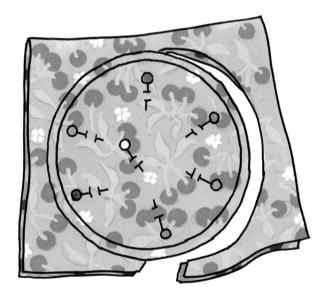

5   Cut along this line through both layers of fabric.

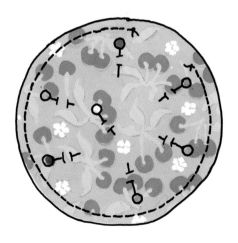

6   Thread a needle and make a beginning knot. Then, using a backstitch, sew the two pieces of fabric together along the sewing line. If you run out of thread before you finish sewing around the circle, make an ending knot. Then rethread the needle, make a beginning knot, and continue sewing.

7 Stop sewing about 4 inches from where you began. Make an ending knot and remove the pins.

8 To avoid having your pillow pucker when you turn it right side out, snip several small wedge-shaped cuts *very slowly and carefully* along the outside edge of your pillow toward the sewing line. Snip as close to it as ⅛ inch, but be *very* careful not to snip across the seam. *(If you snip across the seam it will come apart, making a hole in your pillow, and your fabric will fray. If this happens, thread your needle and make three small, tight, overlapping stitches across the seam about 1 inch from each side of the snip. Cut off the extra thread. Then thread a needle with a new piece of thread and make a beginning knot. Starting from one set of 3 little stitches, backstitch inside the place where you snipped the seam until you reach the second set of 3 little stitches. Make an ending knot.)* Snipping around your pillow is the trickiest part of the project.

9 Turn your pillow right side out.

10 Stuff your pillow through the gap with fiberfill stuffing.

11 Tuck the fabric in around the gap and pin the gap closed.

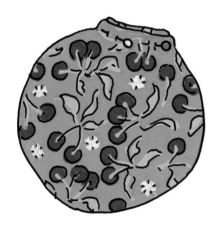

12 Rethread the needle and make a beginning knot. Close the gap with an overhand stitch. When you come to the end of the gap, make a secure ending knot, cut your thread, and take out the pins. Your pillow is done!

your pillow is done!

You can make all kinds of pillows. Choose two different fabrics that look nice together. Use a bigger or smaller bowl, or make another shape by tracing a box or a pan instead. Your pillow will be as beautiful as your stitching and the fabrics you choose. Take your time finding just the right fabrics and making small even stitches.

Draw a heart shape to make a   Heart Pillow

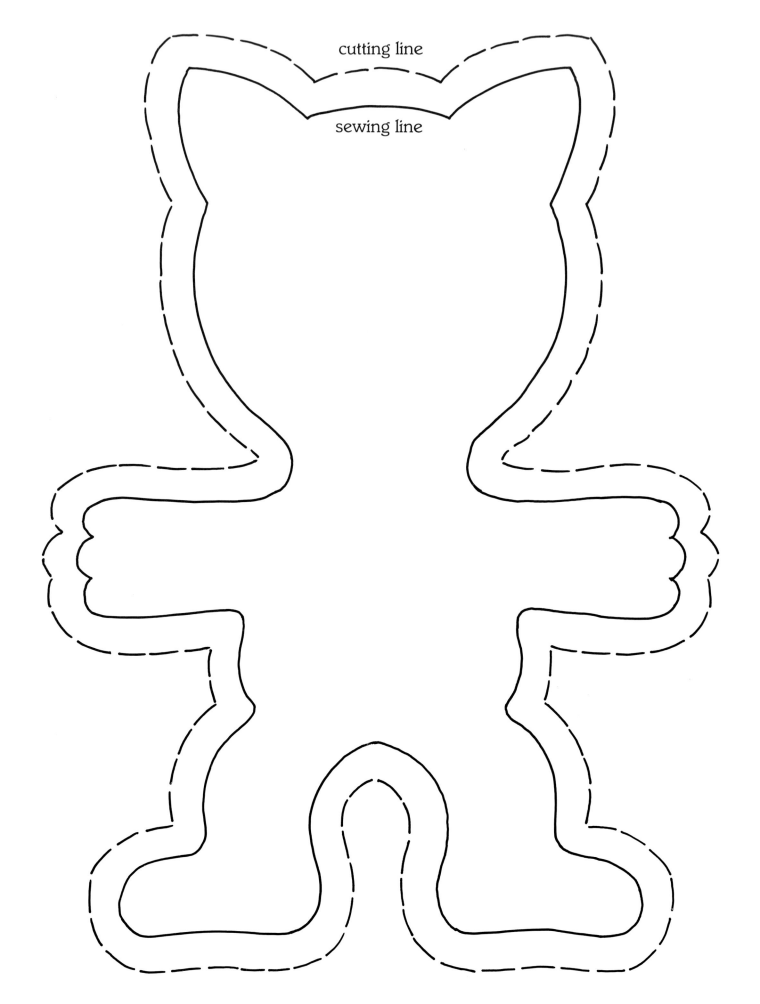

Beanbag Cat

You will need: • ¼ yard of fabric • needle • thread • scissors • pins • dried beans (lentils work well) • pencil • tape measure • tracing paper • buttons • felt

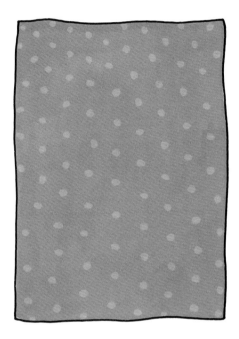

1 Lay your fabric out on a flat surface. Fold one large piece in half or lay two different fabrics together with right sides facing each other. Smooth out any buckles or folds.

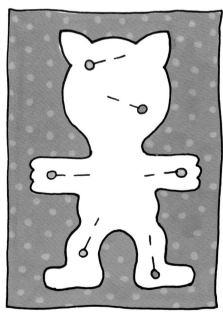

2 Trace the sewing line from the cat pattern onto tracing paper. Cut out your paper pattern and pin it to the fabric.

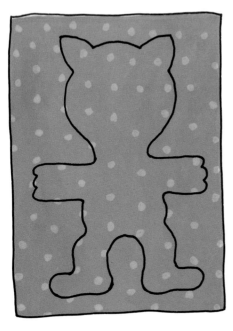

3 Draw with a pencil on your fabric along the edge of your pattern. Remove the pattern.

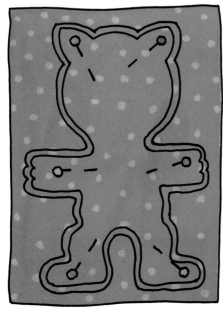

4 Repin the two pieces of fabric together, putting the pins inside the sewing line. Draw a cutting line about ⅜ inch outside the sewing line, by first making several marks and then joining them, as you did with the Circle Pillow.

5 Cut through both pieces of fabric along the cutting line.

6 Sew along the sewing line with a backstitch. Start sewing at the toe or heel of the foot as shown. Make your stitches very small and tight so that the beans can't fall out. Stop sewing about 1½ inches from the end. Knot your thread securely with an ending knot and remove the pins.

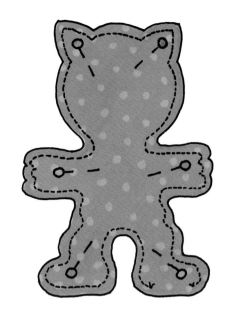

7 *Very slowly and carefully* snip out small wedges along the outside edge toward the sewing line, following the directions in step 8 for the Circle Pillow. Pay special attention at the corners.

8 Turn your cat right side out, using the eraser end of a pencil to push out smaller parts.

9 Fill it with beans. If you want your cat to be nice and floppy, use fewer beans.

10 Pin the gap closed and sew it with an overhand stitch.

Details

Sew on buttons to make eyes and a nose.

1 Mark the spot where you want the button to go.

2 Thread a needle that will fit through the holes in the button and make a beginning knot.

3 Make one small stitch in and out on the spot where you marked your fabric. Pull the thread through so the knot is firmly against the fabric.

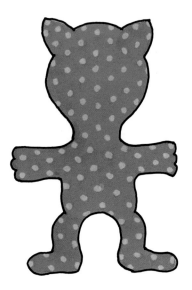

4 If you have a flat button, start from the back of the button, and push your needle in one of the button's holes and back through another. If your flat button has 4

holes, you can make an "x," "=," a square or an arrow design with the thread. If you have a half round or a full round button, just sew through the one hole.

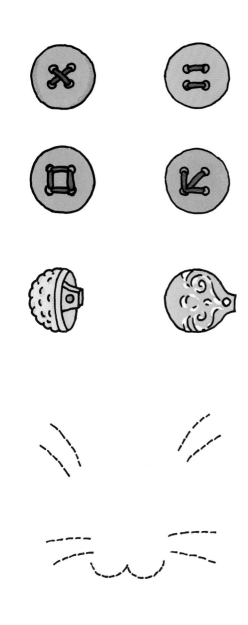

5 Make a stitch in the fabric on top of the first one and pull the button snugly on top of the fabric so that it covers the beginning knot.

6 Repeat these steps several times so the button is secure. Finish with an ending knot. Hide the ending knot under the button.

7 If you want your cat to have whiskers or a mouth, draw with a pencil where you want them to go. Following these lines, sew a backstitch. Repeat the backstitch on top of itself a few times if you want your sewn lines to be thicker. Use felt to make a bowtie.

Now your beanbag cat is ready for lots of flying, hopping, and flopping around!

Beanbag Cat

Draw a bat pattern to make a
Beanbag Bat

This bat is made from
a scrap of black velvet
and has seed pearl eyes.
The stitching between the
body and wings was done
after the bat was stuffed
with beans.

cutting line

sewing line

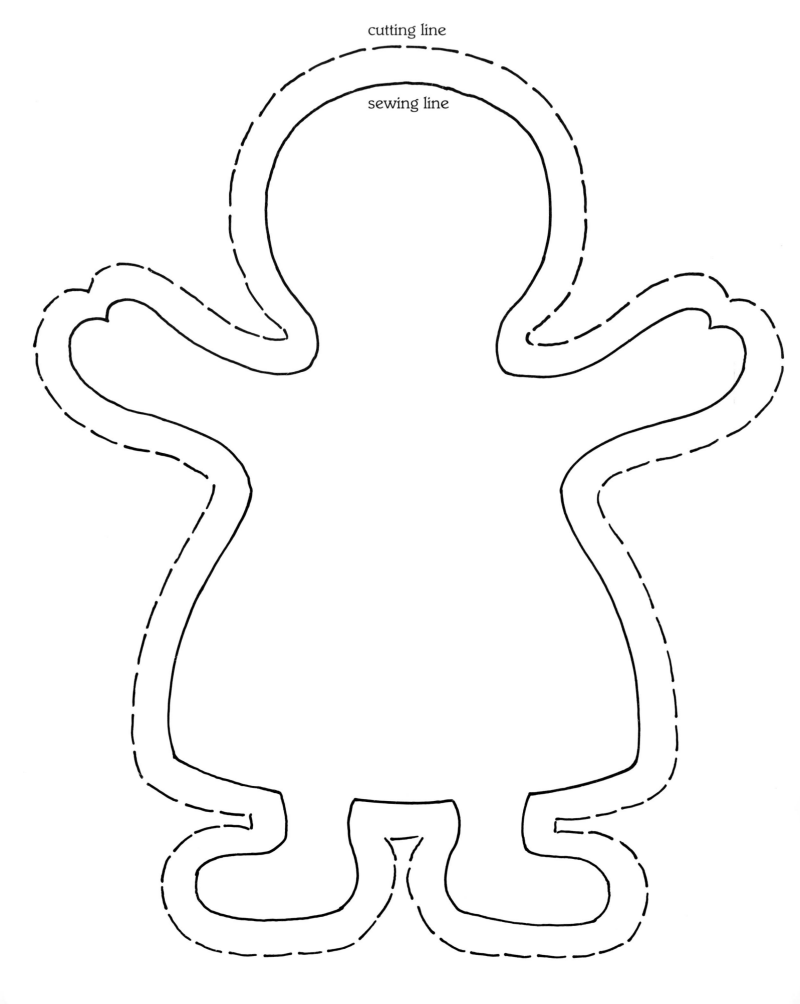

Flower Girl Doll

You will need: • ¼ yard of plain colored fabric • ¼ yard of large floral print • ¼ yard of felt • needle • thread • scissors • pins • pencil • paper • tape measure • fiberfill stuffing • fabric paint • small brush

A Flower Girl Doll is made out of colorful fabric. Her apron and accessories are made from fabric printed with large leaves, flowers, butterflies, or insects.

Start by following steps **1** through **5** of the Beanbag Cat. You may use the doll pattern or make up your own.

6 Sew along the inner line with a backstitch and leave an opening of 1½ inches along the side of her skirt.

7 Cut out wedges along the outside edge. Remember to cut slowly and carefully!

8 Turn your doll right side out, using the eraser end of a pencil or a chopstick to push out smaller parts.

9 Stuff her with fiberfill, starting with small pieces in her hands and feet.

10 When she is nice and round, pin the gap closed and sew with an overhand stitch.

With a pencil draw her eyes, nose and mouth. You may follow these lines with a backstitch or paint them using fabric paint and a small brush.

Apron
You will need: white glue • felt
• scraps of large floral print fabric

1 Choose a flower from the fabric and cut it out, leaving some extra fabric around the edges. Cut out a piece of felt about the same size.

2 Spread glue evenly over the wrong side of the flower. Place it on the felt and smooth it out.

3 Put the flower under a heavy book for about an hour. When it is dry it will be nice and stiff.

4 Cut out your flower shape.

5 Cut a narrow strip of felt about 12 inches long for the sash.

6 Use a running stitch to attach the flower to the sash.

Accessories

Make a hat or purse out of any shape you like in the fabric's design. Sew a hat on your doll's head using a button for an accent. She can have a whole fabric-and-felt wardrobe of flowers, leaves, and insects.

Flower Girl Doll

...and her friends

Change the girl doll pattern to a boy doll pattern, sew on buttons for . . .

Button Boy